W9-AQV-005

What's in that Egg?

Date: 2/14/12

J 591.468 BAI
Baines, Rebecca.
What's in that egg? : a book
about life cycles /

A Book About Life Cycles

BY

BECKY BAINES

PALM BEACH COUNTY
LIBRARY SYSTEM
3650 Summit Boulevard
West Palm Beach, FL 33406-4198

Hey!
What's in that egg?

Hello?
Mom?

Is it a turtle?

Turtles are reptiles. Reptile eggs can be hard but are sometimes soft and leathery. Some reptiles bury their eggs.

A frog?

Frogs are amphibians. Amphibian eggs are like jelly. Some are laid in strings, others in bunches.

They need to stay wet, and are laid in ponds or streams or even in leaves that hold water.

A fish?

Fish lay lots of eggs at a time. Most let their eggs scatter in the water. Some freshwater fish make nests underwater in the sand.

A butterfly?

A butterfly is an insect.
Most insects are tiny.
Insect eggs are teeny tiny
and hidden!

Or a swan?

A swan is a bird.
Birds lay hard-shelled eggs
in nests to keep
them safe.

One thing's for sure, though an egg seems so small ... there's a whole world inside. It's a home after all!

Some babies live in eggs
for only a few days.
Some live there for months.

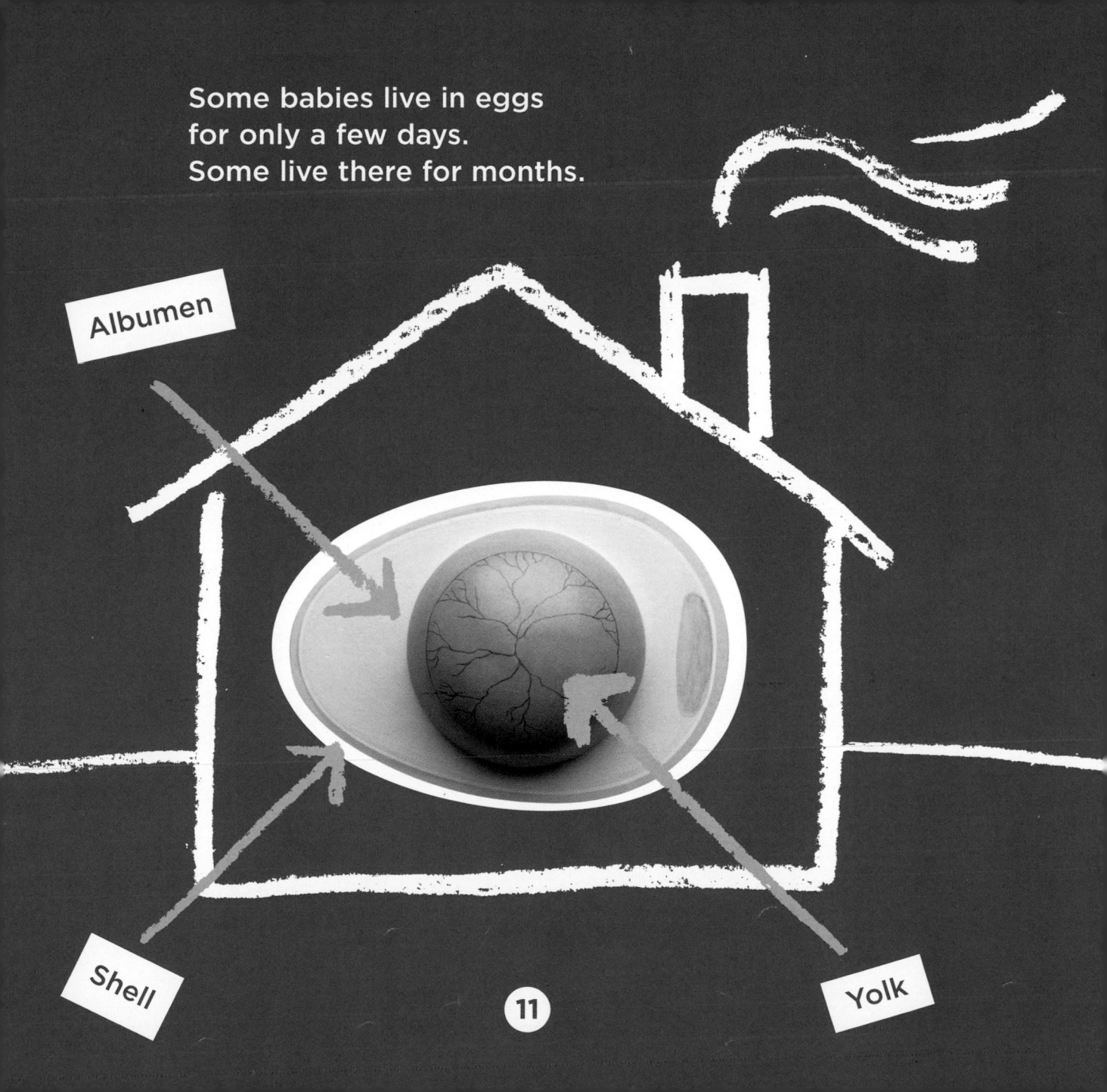

Inside the egg, a baby floats ...

Albumen makes up most of the egg. It allows the growing baby to float and not get bumped around!

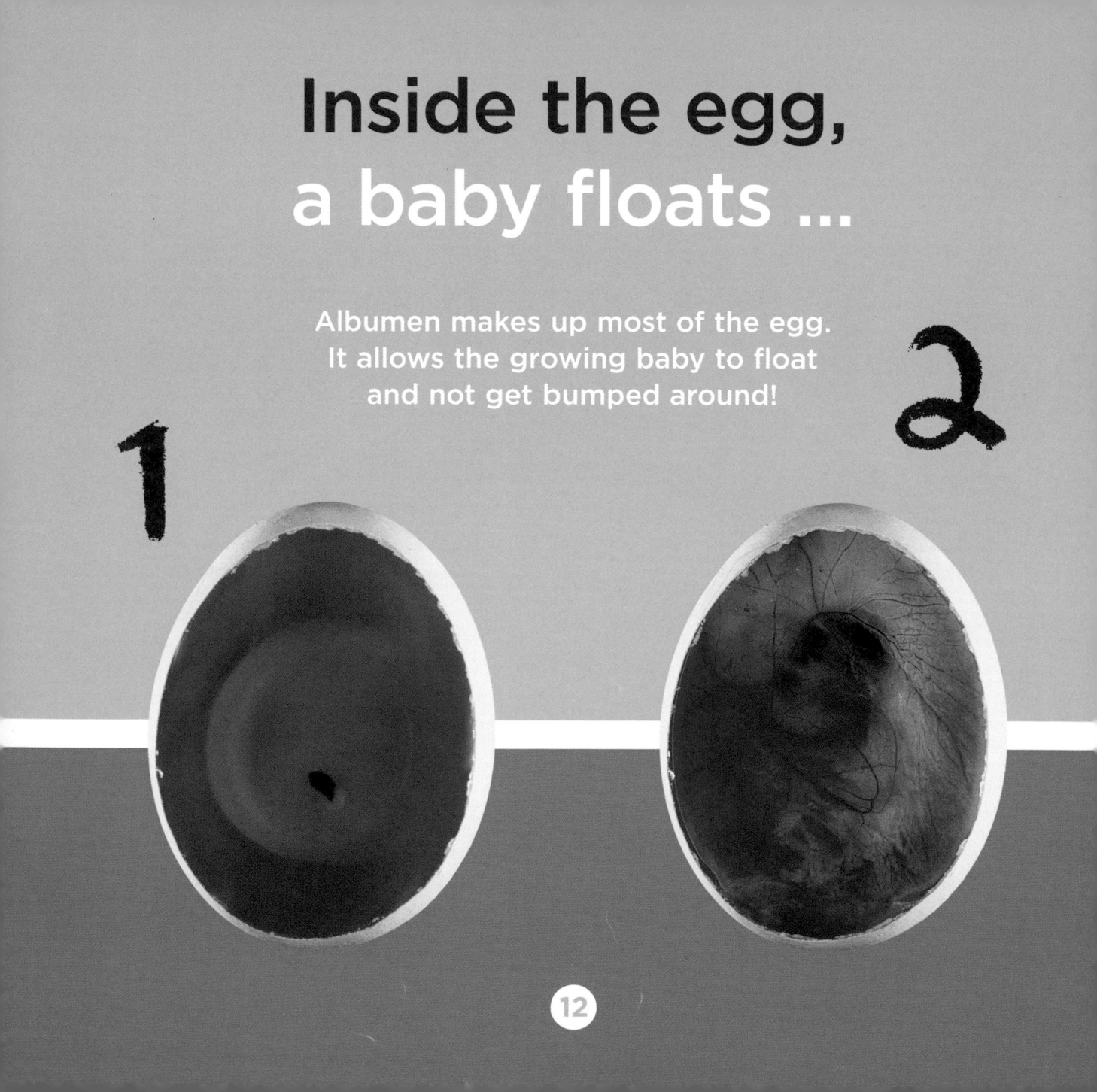

... growing in size while eating the yolk ...

The yolk is the food that the baby eats to make it big and strong.

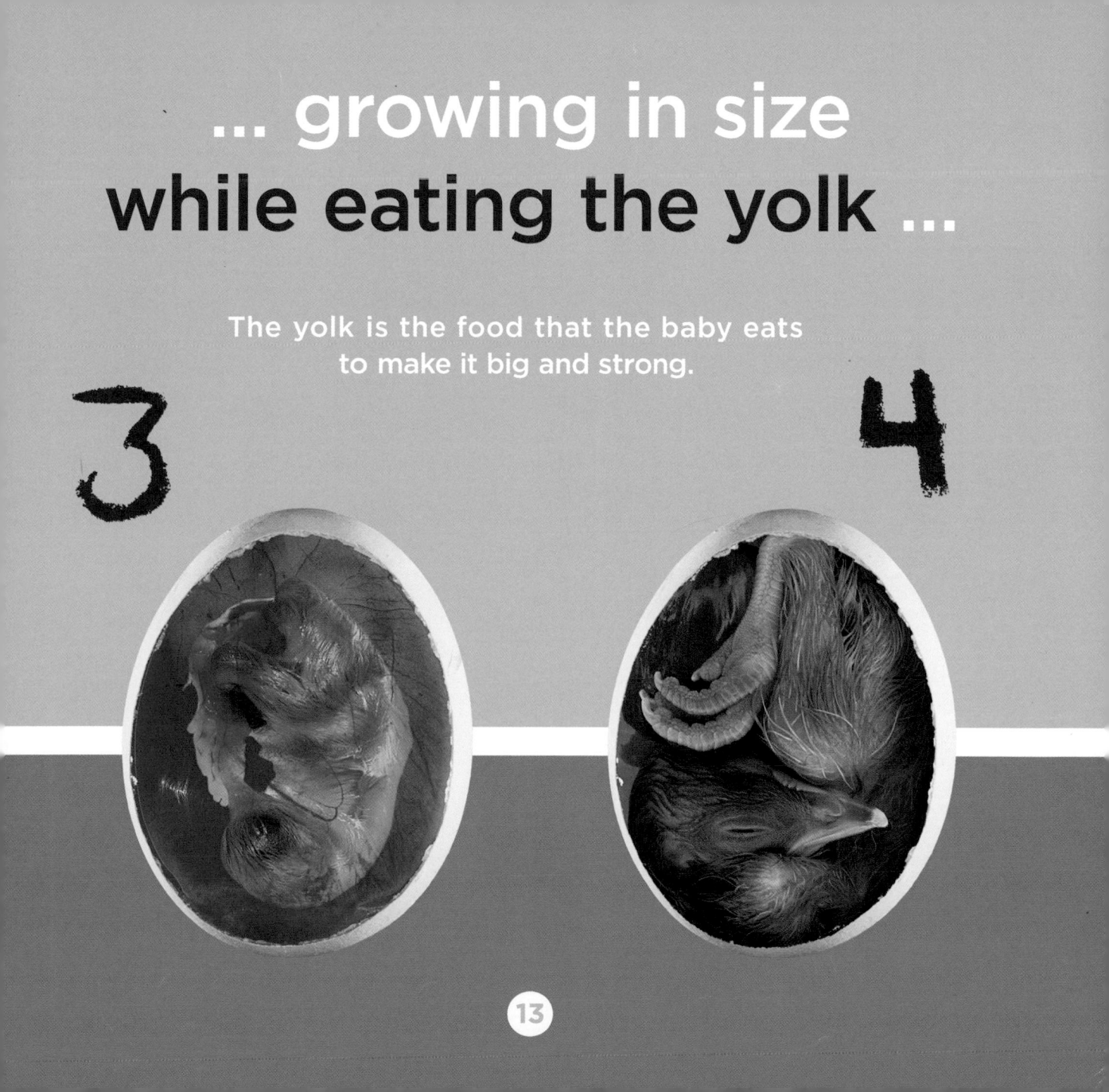

... getting bigger and stronger 'til suddenly ...

... ready or not that egg's going to HATCH!

7

8

Most baby animals "tap" open hard-shelled eggs.

Eggs can be

Apple Snail Eggs

pink!

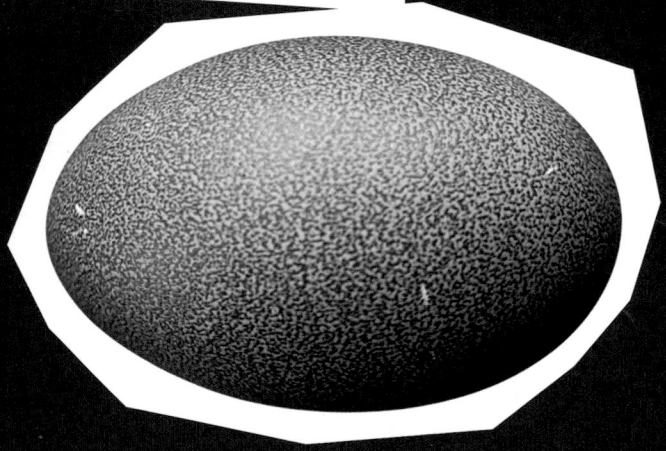

Cassowary Bird Egg

Or green!

Robin Bird Egg

Or blue!

Some eggs can even be see-through!

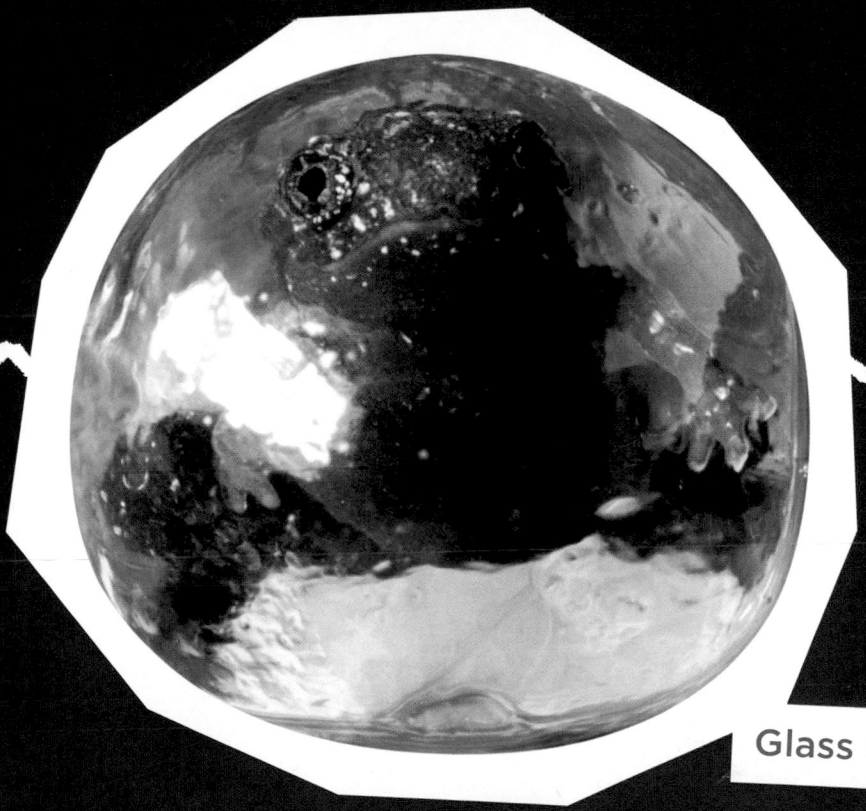

Glass Frog Egg

Long and skinny, pointed or round?

All different shapes of eggs can be found.

Guillemot birds lay their eggs on narrow rock ledges. If the eggs were round, they might roll off the ledge. Their shape keeps them safe.

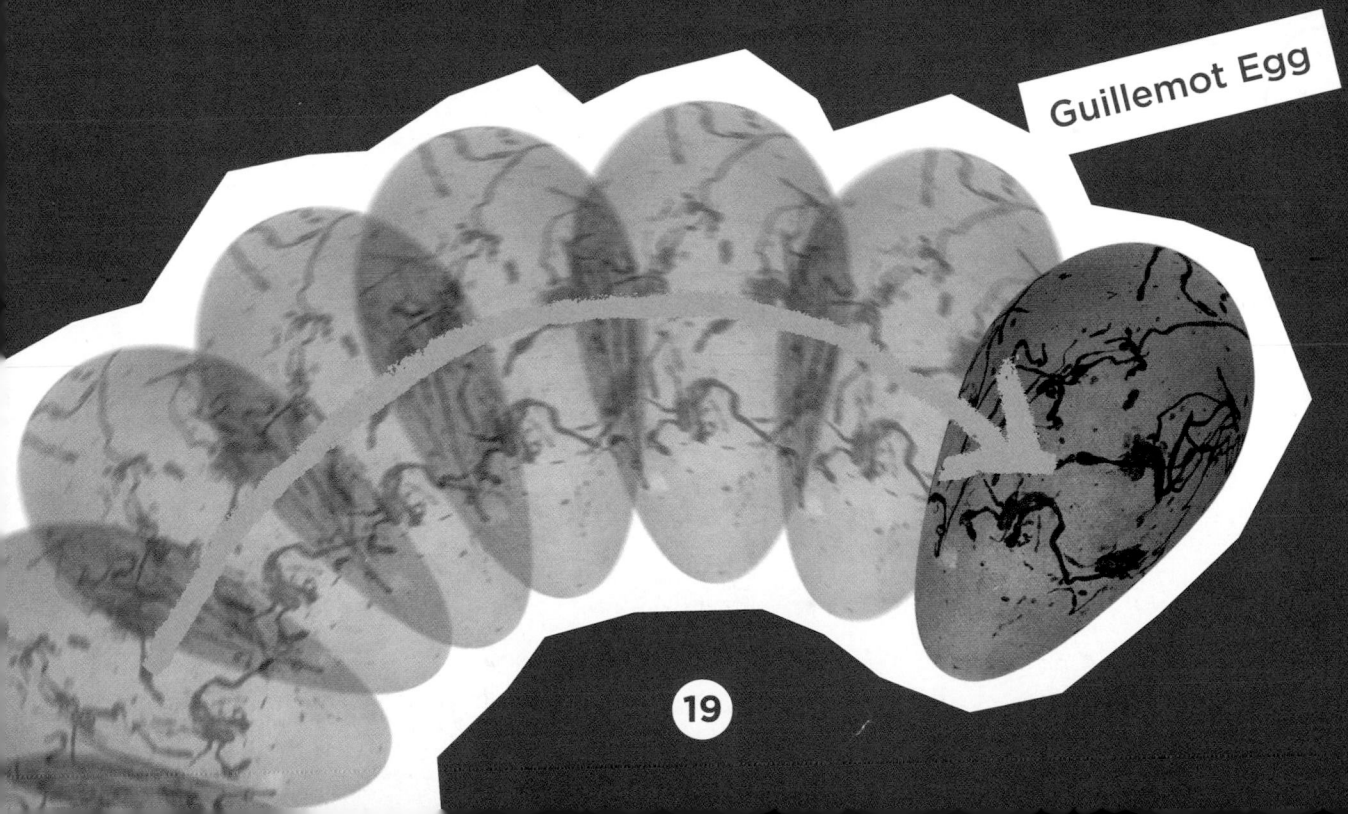

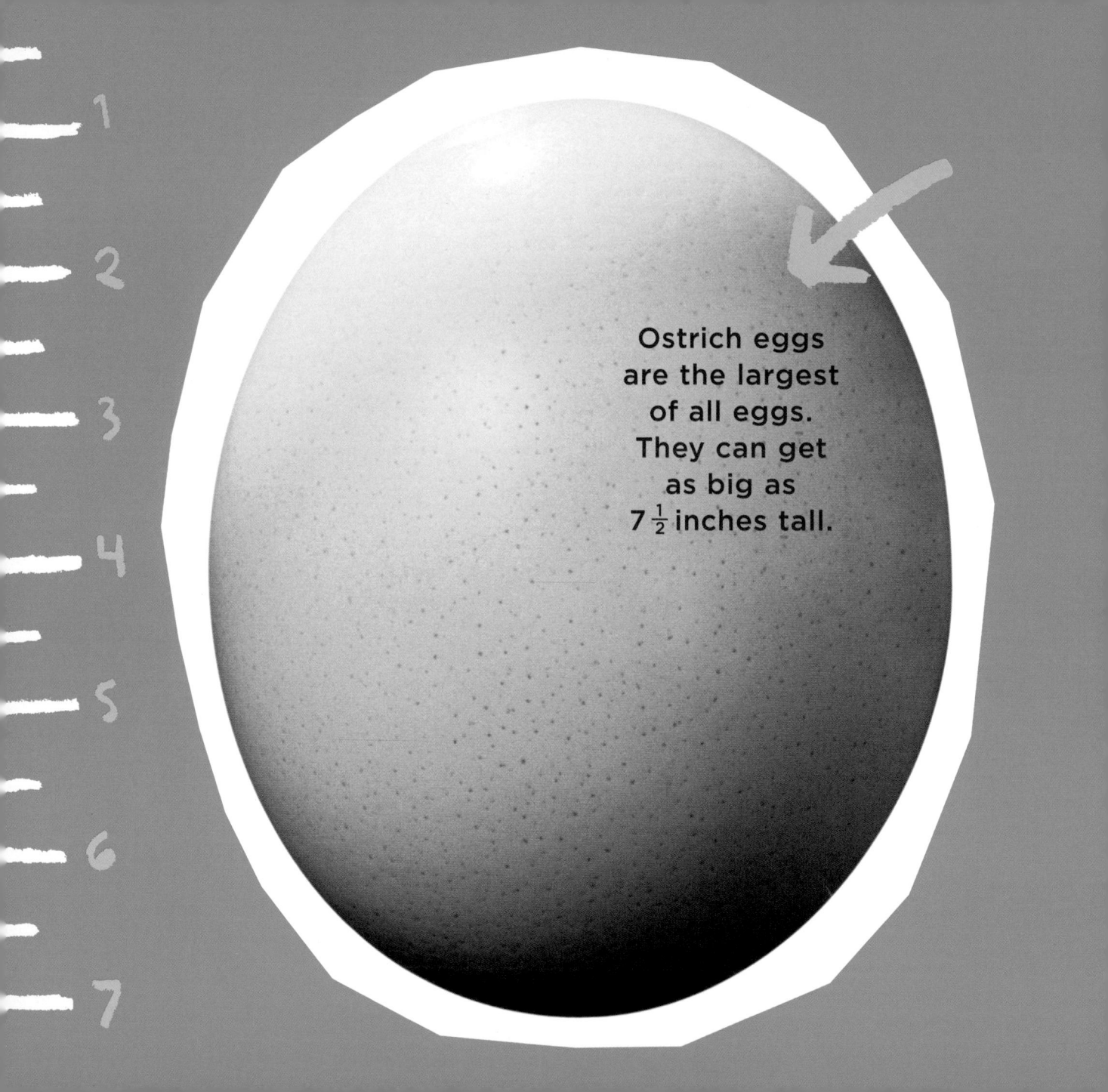

Ostrich eggs are the largest of all eggs. They can get as big as $7\frac{1}{2}$ inches tall.

Bigger than a cantaloupe, or too small to see,

Hummingbirds lay the smallest bird eggs!

They are only about one-half-inch long.

Emperor Penguin Egg

there may be just **one,**

The eggs an animal lays at one time is called a clutch.

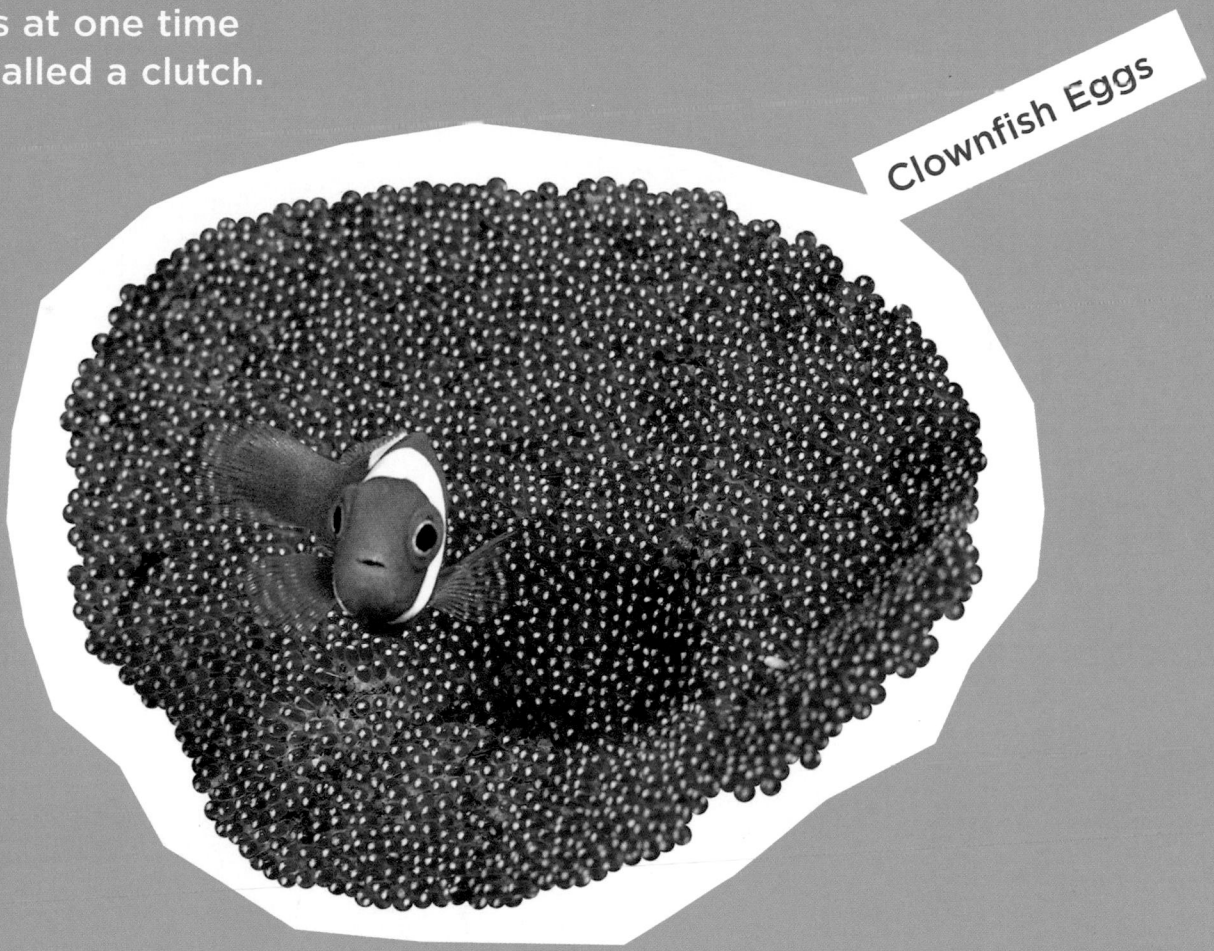

or 2 thousand, or 3!

Is it hard?

Is it soft and leathery?

A baby is born!
Do you know what kind?
The egg might tell
what was growing inside.

Is it underwater?

Is it buried?

Is it teeny tiny?

Is it in a nest?

Is it long and skinny?

Happy Birthday, Alligator!

Alligators are reptiles.

They have soft and leathery eggs, which they bury under leaves or sand.

Zigzag through these ideas for more thoughts about life cycles.

Cut open a hard-boiled egg. The white is the albumen, the yellow is the yolk.

Where was your home when you were born?

If you were a bird, what would you build your nest with to keep your egg safe?

How do animals know when it's time to hatch?

If you had an egg, where would you put it to keep it safe?

When you were a baby, what did you eat to get big and strong?

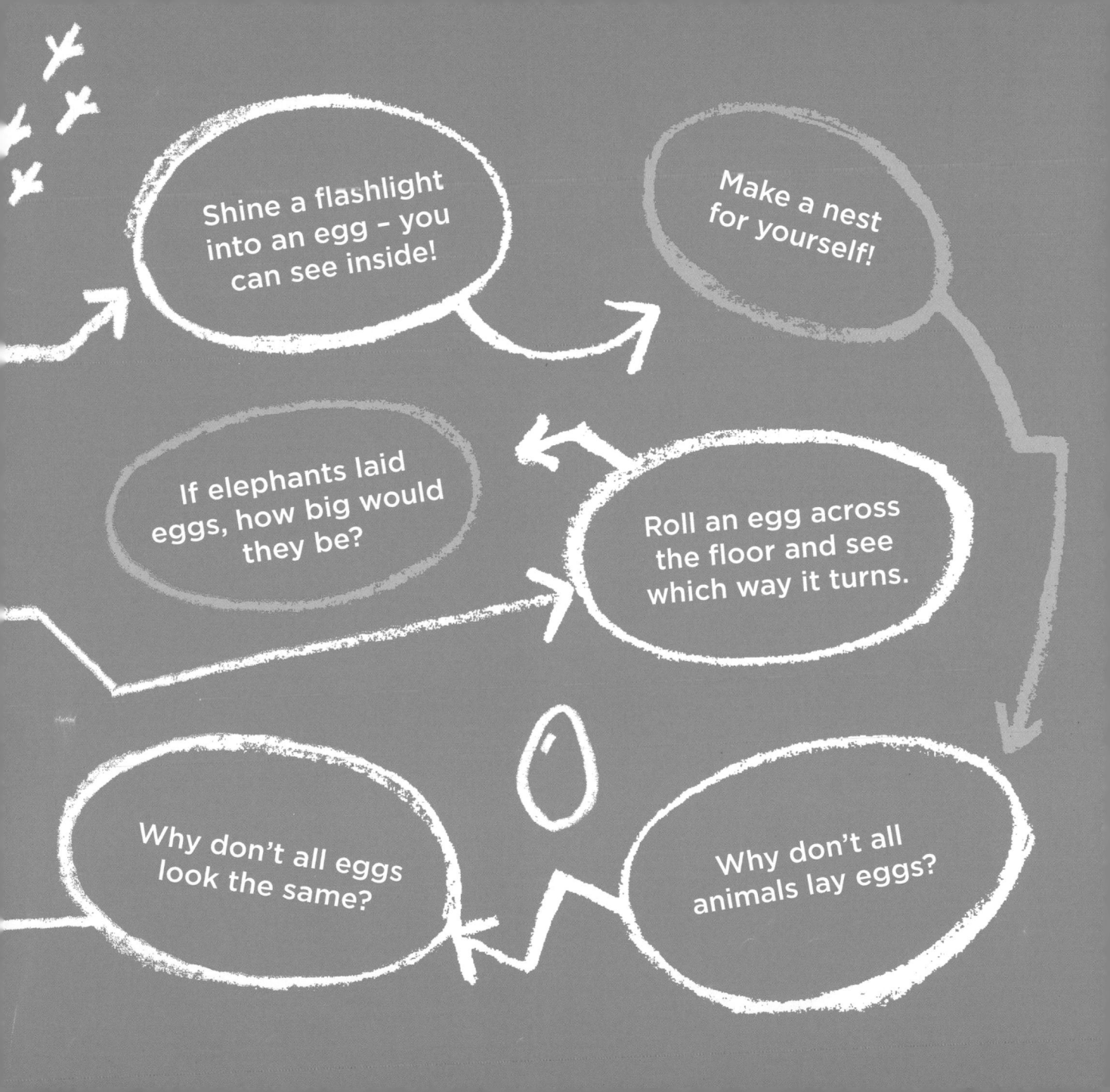
Shine a flashlight into an egg – you can see inside!
Make a nest for yourself!
If elephants laid eggs, how big would they be?
Roll an egg across the floor and see which way it turns.
Why don't all eggs look the same?
Why don't all animals lay eggs?

Copyright ©2009 National Geographic Society. All rights reserved. Reproduction of the whole or any part of the contents without written permission from the publisher is prohibited.

National Geographic's net proceeds support vital exploration, conservation, research, and education programs.

Published by the National Geographic Society
1145 17th Street, N.W.
Washington, D.C. 20036
Visit us online at www.nationalgeographic.com/books

Design: fuszion

Printed in the United States of America

Library of Congress Cataloging-in-Publication Data

Baines, Rebecca.
What's in that egg? : a book about life cycles / by Becky Baines.
p. cm.
ISBN 978-1-4263-0408-8 (hardcover : alk. paper)—
ISBN 978-1-4263-0409-5 (library binding : alk. paper)
1. Embryology—Juvenile literature. 2. Eggs—Juvenile literature. I. Title.
QL956.5.B35 2009
591.4'68--dc22
2008047895

Photo Credits
Corbis: 7, 8, 12, 13, 16, 18, 19, 20, 21, 27
DK Images: 5, 11
Getty: 14, 15, 25
iStock: 9, 18
Jupiter: 6, 22, 30
Minden Pictures: 17
Nature Picture Library: 26
Sea Pics: 23

To Johnny & Liz
- a couple of
good eggs.
—B.B.